D1824574

IN HISTORY
SEA TRANSPORT

Authors:

David Smith and Derek Newton

Illustrated by E. A. Hodges

SCHOFIELD & SIMS LTD., HUDDERSFIELD

© 1972 Schofield & Sims Ltd.

0 7217 1550 8
0 7217 1580 X   Net edition

Printed in England by W. S. Cowell Ltd., at the Butter Market, Ipswich.

First impression 1972
Second impression 1972
Third impression 1974
Fourth impression 1978

Paddling a log

The First Boats

Dug-outs

No one knows when the first boat was made. The first man to venture onto water probably did so sitting astride a log, pushing himself along by using his hands. Man then thought he would be safer and more comfortable if he hollowed out the middle of the log. He used heated stones to char the wood and soften it so that he could hack the middle out with stone saws and axes. Later he found he could travel faster if he used a short pole with a flattened end. This was called a paddle. The hollowed-out log was called a 'dug-out'. Dug-outs, over 20 metres long and 3 metres wide, have been found.

Dug-out canoe

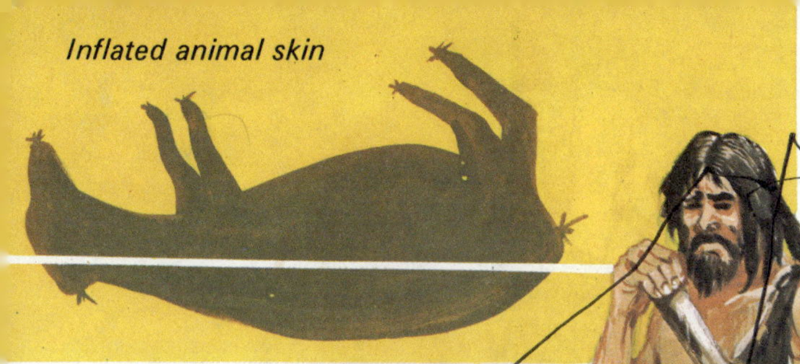

Inflated animal skin

Coracle

Reed boat

Skin Boats

Where there were no tall trees for the making of dug-outs other materials had to be used. Three thousand years ago the Assyrians and Babylonians floated across the River Tigris on animal skins inflated with air. They also used the 'coracle'. This was a framework of branches or woven basketwork which was covered with hide.

When the Romans came to Britain in 55 B.C. they found the Celts using coracles. Coracles are still used in Britain but the framework is now covered with tarred sail-cloth. On the River Tigris a coracle called a 'guffa' is still used.

Reed Boats

Bundles of reeds were sometimes tied together with creepers to make a simple raft. By 4000 B.C. the Egyptians were making large reed rafts. The ends of these rafts were bound together to make them pointed and they curved upwards above the water.

There are similar vessels on Lake Tana in Ethiopia. These are nearly 12 metres long and can carry a load of up to 3000 kilos.

3

Egyptian Ships

These early boats could hardly be called ships. The first seagoing ships we know of were built by the Egyptians. Large reed boats could not be built as they were not firm enough to carry heavy loads. The only wood available was from the small acacia tree and only short planks could be cut from this tree. These short planks were fastened end to end, using wooden pegs or 'dovetail' joints. In this way ships over 30 metres long could be built. These ships were the same shape as the reed rafts. They curved upwards at each end, so that the bow and stern were high out of the water.

Short planks

The Egyptian ships had no keel. A keel is a long piece of timber which acts as a backbone and strengthens the ship. A ship without a keel tends to sag at each end. To prevent this the Egyptians used a 'hogging truss'. A thick rope was fastened to each end of the ship and was supported along the length of the hull by short poles. Another pole was inserted in the middle of the rope and by twisting it the rope was tightened. In this way the ship was strengthened.

Early Egyptian ships had a twin-legged mast which could be lowered when not needed. But by 1500 B.C. they had a single pole mast, set amidships. Ropes, called 'shrouds', held the mast in position. When there was no wind the ship was propelled by oarsmen who rowed standing up. An overseer with a whip saw that they did not slacken, and two men in the bows beat out a steady rhythm on two sticks called 'sounding rods'. This ensured the oarsmen worked together as a team. The pair of steering oars at the stern were turned by using a 'tiller'.

Cretan and Phoenician Ships

Crete

The Cretans were the first people to develop two distinct types of ship, namely, trading vessels called 'round' ships, and fighting ships called 'long' ships. The trading ships, shorter and wider, could hold a lot of cargo and often they relied on their square mainsail only.

Bireme

The Galley

The warship was long and narrow with a sharp ram at the bow. It was driven by many rowers who were seated on long benches. This type of ship was called a 'galley'.

Phoenicia

The Phoenicians also had trading ships and galleys. They developed the 'bireme' which was a galley with two banks of oars, one above the other. The Phoenician galleys had a strong keel and were up to 40 metres long and 7 metres wide. There was little room for food and water, but ships were sailed only during the day, and were beached for the night. They were steered with two rudders near the stern.

Arrangement of oars

Trireme

Greek Ships

The Trireme

The Greeks copied the Phoenician galley. They developed a warship called a 'trireme'. This had three banks of oars, one above another. The oarports were covered with leather to keep water out.

Arrangement of oars

Merchant Ships

The Greeks had trading vessels. They were shorter than the galleys and much broader and deeper. The sides of the deck were raised to protect the cargo which was covered with matting. These merchant ships were too big to be beached, so sheltered harbours were needed and anchors were used to prevent the ships from drifting.

The Greeks used simple maps and charts of those parts of the world which were known to them.

Trading ship

7

Ancient Roman Ships

Roman Galleys

The Roman fighting ships were galleys. The Roman ship had a smaller ram about 2 metres above the main ram so that in a fight a larger hole was torn in the enemy ship. At the stern was a deckhouse to shelter the ship's officers. A raised centre gangway was used by the officers as they supervised the rowers. In the bow was another raised platform where soldiers stood. As the Romans were not great sailors they tried to make a sea battle as much like a land battle as possible by boarding the enemy ship and engaging in hand-to-hand fighting. They used a heavy plank with a spiked end. It was called a 'corvus'. When the ship was close enough to the enemy, one end of the corvus was dropped on the deck of the enemy ship. The hook held the boarding plank securely and the soldiers ran across to fight their enemy. The Romans also used catapults to hurl stones.

Roman Merchantmen

Roman merchantmen were used mainly to bring corn from Egypt to Rome. By A.D. 100 these corn ships had two masts. The mainmast had a large square sail, and a smaller foremast called a 'dolon' stood out from the bow at an angle. This held a small sail called an 'artemon'. Sometimes the mainmast carried a small topsail as well. The artemon was useful in catching a side wind and helping control the ship. The mainsail had many shrouds which allowed the helmsman to turn the ship's sail sideways to catch the wind.

The ship had a large deckhouse at the stern and there was a cargo hatch in the deck.

Roman corn ships were up to 30 metres long and about 9 metres wide. They could carry more than two hundred and fifty people and transport up to two hundred and fifty tonnes of cargo.

Roman merchantman

9

Northern Ships

The development in northern ships began in Scandinavia. By the year 1000 B.C. the Scandinavians had huge dug-outs. One dug-out, found in 1886, was almost 16 metres long. The Scandinavians found that if they lashed a plank on each side of a dug-out it gave them more room and protection. When they added another plank on each side slightly overlapping the first, they had a very seaworthy boat. By A.D. 250 boats with five overlapping planks on each side were being built. The original log formed a very strong keel. The planks were fastened together with iron nails. The sharp end of each nail was hammered over a joint so that it clinched the two planks together like a rivet.

The Vikings

The kind of ship used by the Vikings was pointed at both ends. These ends rose high out of the water and often had fierce faces carved on them. The Viking longship was very narrow and could sail in shallow water. The earliest Viking ships had no mast but relied on their oars. Later, a mast was added so that a large square sail could be raised by using a simple windlass.

When the wind was unfavourable the mast was taken down and, with the sail spread over it, it provided shelter for the crew. The oarsmen rowed standing up and there were as many as sixteen of them on each side. The oarports could be covered with wooden shutters. A Viking ship was steered with a large steer-oar on the right-hand side of the ship. This side of the ship with the steer-oar came to be called the starboard side.

At Gokstad in Norway a Viking ship dated about A.D. 900 has been found. This ship is like those in which the Vikings sailed to raid England. She is just over 25 metres long and about 5·5 metres wide.

Viking ship

Arrangement
of planks

Figurehead

Old coin
showing Viking ship

Stern and
steer-oar

11

Saxon and Norman Ships

The Saxon and Norman ships were double-ended and clinker-built like those of the Vikings, but they were much larger and wider. They were so heavy they were difficult to row, so they came to rely on the sail only and dispensed with the oars. Long shrouds were fastened from the upper part of the sail to the sides of the ship. This gave extra support to the mast in strong winds.

Fastened to the bottom of the sail was a rope called a 'sheet'. This was held by the helmsman. By hauling on this rope he could turn the sail to catch side winds. The ships had little or no decking. Passengers were exposed to cold and wet and the cargo was easily damaged by salt water. A Norman ship could carry as many as three hundred people.

Norman ship

Dromon

Mediterranean Ships

When the Crusaders sailed into the Mediterranean they were amazed to see the two- and three-masted warships of the Saracens. The Saracen warships had triangular sails called 'lateen' sails. The Saracens copied this idea from the Arab ships in the Indian Ocean, which had had triangular sails since about A.D. 800. With triangular sails a ship could sail closer to the wind and tack more easily. Merchant ships carried one lateen sail on a single mast.

The most fearsome Saracen warship was the 'dromon'. It had up to three masts with lateen sails, as well as oars on each side of the ship. There were two or three rudders near the stern and the hull was covered with leather. It was said to hold

Arab dhow

one thousand five hundred men.

The galley was still popular in the Mediterranean, and it was in this sea that sailors first used the magnetic compass. A magnetised needle, floating in a bowl of water, gave a rough guide to direction. However, it was not popular with Northern sailors who thought it was witchcraft.

13

The Middle Ages

Castle Ships

In the Northern seas there was no difference between a warship and a merchant ship. In wartime, carpenters fitted wooden castles at the bow and stern of merchant ships. These castles were called the 'forecastle' and the 'aftercastle'. The aftercastle later came to be called the 'poop'. On the top of the mast was a platform called the 'fighting-top'. Archers and fighting men occupied the castles during a battle. These castles became a permanent part of the ship, for the forecastle provided shelter in heavy seas and the high poop gave additional cabin space.

Castle ships with quarter rudder

The Stern Rudder

Until the thirteenth century ships were double-ended. Then it was realised that a ship could be more easily steered if the steer-oar was fastened to the stern only. This type of steer-oar was called a 'rudder', and the shape of the stern was altered so that the rudder could be more easily fixed. A short spar was also placed in the bow. Lines from this 'bowsprit' were attached to the sail so that it could be turned sideways.

The Cog and the Nef

By the middle of the thirteenth century there were two main kinds of ship, the larger 'cog' with its stern rudder, and the 'nef' with its quarter rudder. Decks and cabins were more common and life at sea was rather more comfortable. During the fourteenth century pumps were introduced into ships to clear away bilge water. Sea voyages were very short and so fresh food was plentiful. Seamen were often part-owners of their ships and shared the profits of a voyage. Discipline was strict but not severe. A sailor could be whipped but no blood had to be drawn. If he struck his captain he could choose between losing a hand or being fined.

In wartime a separate crew of soldiers came on board.

By 1400 the single-masted, square-sailed ships had been improved but they were still little more than coasters, and sailors were afraid to sail out of sight of land.

Cog with stern rudder

15

Fifteenth-century Changes

The Caravel

Henry V, King of Portugal, wanted to find a sea route to India round the coast of Africa. He realised that the single-masted, square-sailed Northern ships were not suitable for ocean voyages. He studied the Mediterranean ships and adopted the idea of three masts carrying lateen sails. The result was the 'caravel'. She carried a fore-mast, a mainmast, and a stern or mizzen-mast, each with a lateen sail. Room was made for living quarters for the crew, and for cargo and food supplies. The ship had three main sections — the 'high bow', the 'stern', and there was also the 'lower waist' where the cargo and supplies could be stored.

The Carrack

The caravel was the best for sailing in side winds, but she lost the advantage of the large square mainsail in a following wind. Other ship designers preferred to have both kinds of sails. The 'carrack' had square sails on the fore and mainmasts and a lateen sail on the mizzen-mast. Later, a small extra sail was put beneath the bow-sprit, called a 'water sail', and the foremast was moved further back to take more sail. The masts were too tall for one sail so the fore and mainmasts each had two sails.

By 1486 ships had what was called the 'six-sail rig' — water-sail, foresail and fore-topsail, mainsail and main-topsail, and mizzen-sail. This basic design was to survive until the clipper ships of the nine-teenth century.

Navigational Aids

Sailors now used a simple compass. It was a box containing a card with 32 points of the compass on it, and a needle-shaped bar magnet. This was set in a bowl of water so that it swung freely. They also had the 'astrolabe' which could be used to find the latitude by giving the height above the horizon of the sun or the pole-star. Time was measured with a half-hour sandglass.

Astrolabe

Caravel

Compass

Carrack

Sandglass

17

Mediterranean Developments

The merchants of Venice and Genoa also adopted the carrack as a trading vessel. The galley survived as a fighting ship in the Mediterranean for several hundred years. Both the French and the Spaniards used galleys in the Mediterranean. They were rowed by convicts. The galley was also popular with the pirates of the North African coast. Their galleys had one or two masts carrying lateen sails.

The living quarters for the officers were at the stern, while at the bow there was a platform for soldiers. Projecting from the bow was a ram. When cannon were introduced onto ships these galleys carried them in the forward bulkhead so that they could fire forward.

The Venetians had beautiful state galleys and a large war galley called a 'galeass' which had three lateen sails.

War galley

Mediterranean galley

Early cannon

Gun-ports

Tudor Ships

Although ships grew in size and more sail was carried, the basic sail plan of three masts remained, except for the occasional use of a fourth mast called a 'bonaventure'. Some ships now had as many as six decks. The next change in ships was caused by the improvement in cannon.

Cannon

Cannon had been carried on ships as early as 1311. These were clumsy breech-loaders fastened to pieces of timber. They were placed in the castles of the ship and were few in number. For sufficient guns to be carried to sink an enemy ship, they had to be placed low down in the hull so that they protruded through the timbers. But this meant cutting holes in the hull close to the waterline. A Frenchman, Descharges, was the first to do this in 1501.

Bonaventure mast

In 1545 an English ship called the *Mary Rose*, which had gun-ports fitted in her hull, sank like a stone as water rushed in through the gun-ports during a storm.

Great Ships or Galleons

However, cannon on board ships had come to stay. A special balk of timber called the 'gunwale' was fitted to support the heavy cannon.

Ships were now built to hold as many guns as possible. They were called 'great ships' or 'galleons', and were really just floating gun-platforms.

King Henry VIII of England had the *Henri Grâce à Dieu* or *Great Harry* built in 1514. She was a three-decker with eight decks on the poop and she carried one hundred and eighty-six guns.

Each maritime nation had at least one great ship. France had the *Grande Fran-coise,* Scotland the *Great Michael,* and Sweden the *Elefant.* These ships caused a change in naval tactics. The captain tried to turn his ship broadside on to the enemy to bring as many guns to bear as possible.

Henri Grâce à Dieu

Elizabethan galleon

Swivel gun

Elizabethan Galleon

Great ships were only suitable for close fighting in the Channel. They sailed very slowly and could not manoeuvre quickly.

An English sailor, Sir John Hawkins, helped design a slimmer, smaller galleon. Because of her shape she was faster through the water and could bring her guns to bear quickly.

She still had a high stern but the bow was much lower in the water. Projecting from the bow was a huge beak which prevented a head sea from sweeping through the ship. This beak was often decorated with a figurehead.

The Elizabethan galleon usually carried only one row of guns but she had swivel guns in the forecastle and poop to repel boarders. Queen Elizabeth's warships were built to this design. It was these ships which defeated the Spanish Armada in 1588. With their superior speed and manoeuvrability they created havoc among the heavy, lumbering Spanish galleons.

21

Life on Board a Tudor Ship

The master and the captain had their cabins under the poop. Their cabins were well stocked with food served from silver plates. Sometimes the captain took musicians to sea so that they could play while he ate.

The other officers had quarters in the 'orlop'. This was an extra short deck at the stern. Some of the crew had their berths in the forecastle but most had their berths below the main deck. These quarters were so evil-smelling and airless that often the sailors slept on deck.

Stores were also kept in the forecastle but most of the stores — food, water, beer and gunpowder — were kept in the ship's hold.

The sailors' clothes were made of canvas or calico. The crew had plenty to eat but the food was of poor quality. Each group of four men received a half kilogramme of bread and four and a half litres of beer each day, with salt meat or fish. On special days they had butter or olive oil. Sailors were paid only a few pence each day, but they also shared in the money received for a captured enemy ship. Punishment was very severe and flogging was common. Bad offenders were shot or hanged.

The Ship's Officers

The ship's chief officers were the captain and the master or navigator. There were also: the gunner in charge of the cannon; the master-at-arms who looked after muskets and pistols; and the boatswain who was responsible for rigging and boats. The coxswain looked after the captain's shore-boat, the quartermaster was responsible for the contents of the hold, and the purser was in charge of the accounts.

Each ship had a carpenter, a sailmaker, a cooper, a chaplain, and a surgeon.

23

Stuart Ships

The Stuart period is often known as the decorative period. All ships were covered with gilt-covered figures and shapes. During a battle this decorative work on warships was protected by padding.

Much more care was taken in the design of ships. Plans and models were made of every important ship before it was built. James I and Charles II were keen to build up the strength of the Royal Navy. As ships continued to increase in size, the number of sails carried also increased. The *Royal Prince,* launched in 1610, was over 43 metres long and 10 metres wide. She was the first British ship to have three covered gun decks. She even had two sails on her bowsprit.

English shipwrights changed the shape of the stern of ships to give them greater stability. They rounded off the planking from the ship's bottom at the stern for about 3 metres. This was called a 'round-tuck' stern. The waist of the ship was higher and the height of the poop was less pronounced.

Royal Prince

Transom stern

Round-tuck stern

24

East Indiamen

East Indiamen

It was still hard to distinguish a merchant ship from a warship, and many merchantmen still carried cannon because of the danger from pirates. The best merchantmen belonged to the East India Company. There was little attempt to increase a ship's speed. The ships were slow, and also very broad in order to hold as much cargo as possible. They had a blunt bow and a very high stern to give extra cabin space so that passengers could be as comfortable as possible. A journey to India and back could take two years. An East Indiaman often had live sheep, hens, turkeys and even cows on board, to provide fresh food for as long as possible.

25

Ship of the Line

Until 1653 warships sailed into battle with no set battle-plan. Then the British Admiralty gave orders that ships should give battle in line, with the largest ships first. This led to ships being classified according to size and number of guns. Ships with one hundred guns were called 'first-rates', those with ninety to one hundred were 'second-rates', and those with sixty to eighty were 'third-rates'.

At the beginning of the eighteenth century the Admiralty forbade the decoration

Ship of the line in battle

of warships. The lines of ships became much simpler, with the forecastle and poop almost at the same height as the waist. English warships were painted in broad, yellow and black stripes.

Improved Navigation

The backstaff and the quadrant invented by John Davis, and the sextant, invented by John Hadley in 1731, enabled sailors to find latitude more accurately. The chronometer, invented by John Harrison in 1761, enabled longitude to be found accurately.

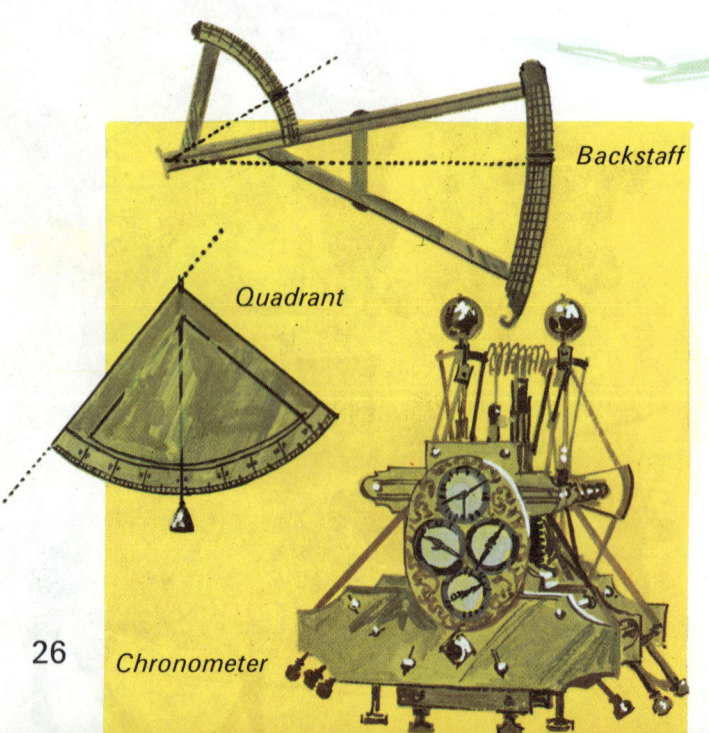

Backstaff

Quadrant

Chronometer

The worst disease was scurvy. This was caused by the lack of wholesome food. A sailor's diet was dried peas or beans made into a watery soup, hard biscuits, and salt pork or fish. On a long voyage the biscuits became full of weevils and the salt pork rotten. There was beer to drink but when it was all consumed the sailors had only water. Water was stored in casks and soon was covered with a green slime. It was discovered that sailors who had a diet of fresh fruit or fruit juice did not catch scurvy, and from 1795 each sailor in the Royal Navy was given a ration of lemon juice.

Service at Sea in the Eighteenth Century

Discipline on board ship was severe and flogging was very common. There were also the dangers of being washed overboard or falling from the rigging during a storm. Older seamen looked after the lower sails while younger seamen, called 'topmen', looked after the rigging aloft.

On a long voyage disease was common. Often half the crew died from sickness. The ship's decks were washed down with vinegar, and sulphur was burned below deck to try to keep down harmful germs.

Reefing sail

27

Sometimes chickens, cows and goats were kept on deck to provide fresh eggs and milk. However, during the first serious storm the chickens would be drowned and the cows and goats so badly injured that they would have to be killed.

Not surprisingly, few men volunteered for service at sea. There were three services available; the Merchant Service, the East India Company, and the Royal Navy.

The East India Company recruited sailors without much trouble for they tried to treat them fairly, and gave them the best food possible. They paid a sailor's wife regularly while he was away, and if he died or was killed his widow and orphans received a pension.

In the Merchant Service there were good ships and bad ships. The captain of a bad ship had great difficulty in getting a crew. Lodging house and tavern keepers drugged sailors or got them drunk and then handed them over to sea captains who put to sea before the men recovered.

The Royal Navy

Conditions in the Royal Navy were the worst of all. Dishonest contractors who supplied the ships bribed the officers to accept poor quality supplies and food, which was usually rotten even before the ships put to sea.

To get crews, convicts and gaol-birds were drafted into the Navy. Sometimes an East Indiaman would be boarded and its crew taken.

The Press Gang

The Navy also had the 'Right to Press'. A group of sailors called the 'Press Gang' went ashore with an officer. Any able-bodied men would be seized and dragged aboard ship as new crew members.

Frigate and Clipper

During the American War of Independence the Americans designed fast, well-armed 'frigates'. These ships were about five times as long as they were wide. They had three tall masts, each carrying four sails. The design of the 'clipper' was based upon the American frigate. The first clipper ships were designed to take people on a quick passage round Cape Horn to the Californian goldfields, a journey of over nineteen thousand kilometres which took ninety days. Some clipper ships were six times as long as they were wide. They had very tall masts carrying as many as seven sails each, as well as many extra sails. It is said that the first American clipper ship was The *Rainbow*, launched in 1845.

Ariel and Taeping racing up Channel

Rainbow

The clipper ships were also used to bring tea from China to America. One ship delivered a cargo of tea to London. The time taken for its voyage astonished British ship-owners.

The Tea Races

The shipping of tea from China developed into a race to land the first crop of the season which brought a very high price. British ship owners needed fast ships and they bought American clippers until they developed their own. The first British clipper ship was the *Challenger*. Between 1863 and 1869 many fast clipper ships were built, like the *Taeping, Ariel, Thermopylae* and *Cutty Sark.*

Fast Liners

Speed became very important as more people wanted to travel. The East Indiamen were redesigned for speed by the builders of the Blackwall frigates.

The American 'Black Ball' line set up the first regular transatlantic service. Their ships sailed to a regular timetable. With five sails on each mast, they sailed from London to New York in thirty-three days and back in twenty-one days. Until 1850 they were the quickest and cheapest form of sea travel.

The sailing ship, however, was soon to have a serious rival in the steamship. On the Tea Run to China the clipper was supreme, until the opening of the Suez Canal in 1869. This greatly reduced the length of a sea-journey to the East, but the canal route could not be used by sailing ships.

The clippers were switched to carrying wool from Australia to England, but on this route, too, they were soon replaced by steamers.

Comet

Charlotte Dundas

Clermont

Early Steamers

Early experimental steamers were built by Jonathan Halls in 1736 and John Fitch in 1787, but the first of the modern steamships was the *Charlotte Dundas* built in 1802 by William Symington. She had a steam-driven paddle wheel and was designed to be used on the Forth–Clyde Canal.

Robert Fulton, an American, built the *Clermont* which had two paddle wheels. In 1807 she began a regular passenger service between New York and Albany.

In 1812 a Scot, Henry Bell, launched the *Comet*. She had two paddle wheels and her smoke-stack was tall enough to carry a sail. She began a regular passenger service on the River Clyde.

By 1815 there were steamers on the Thames, and by 1820 there was a service across the English Channel.

Across the Atlantic

In 1819 the *Savannah*, a sailing ship with a steam engine and paddle wheels, crossed the Atlantic. She used her sails for most of the twenty-nine and a half day voyage but for eighty hours she used her steam engine.

A steamship service would be more reliable than sail, but the problem was how to carry enough fuel for the voyage and still have room for passengers or cargo.

Isambard K. Brunel, the engineer for the Great Western Railway, persuaded his company to build a steamer, the *Great Western*. While she was being built, a steamer, the *Sirius*, left Liverpool on April 5th 1858. She crossed the Atlantic in eighteen days and ten hours, but to do this she had to burn spars, planking and even furniture to keep the engine going.

The *Great Western*, which was fitted with an engine which burned less coal, crossed the Atlantic in fifteen days without mishap, and proved the steamship to be reliable.

Great Western

Sirius

33

Iron Ships

As long as ships were made of wood there was a limit to their size. A large wooden ship would need timber so thick that it would be unmanageable. Experiments were carried out with iron ships and in 1822 the first iron ship, the *Aaron Manby*, was built.

In 1834 an iron ship, the *Garry Owen*, went on the rocks with several wooden ships. While the wooden ships were battered to pieces the *Garry Owen* survived.

Screw Propellers

There were also experiments to find a different way of driving ships, because in a bad storm paddles were liable to be lifted out of the water and become damaged. In 1838 a successful 'screw-propeller' was designed by Francis Smith, a Middlesex farmer, and Captain John Ericsson, a Swedish soldier living in England. The superiority of the screw-propeller was approved when the British Admiralty arranged a contest between the *Rattler*, a screw-driven ship, and the *Alecto*, a paddle-steamer. The two ships were lashed stern to stern and the *Rattler* towed the *Alecto* backwards. Shipbuilders switched to screw propellers.

Alecto

Rattler

34

An iron ship which amazed the world was the *Great Eastern*. She was 227 metres long with five funnels and six masts, and she had both paddle wheels and screw-propellers.

Steamships were now reliable enough to challenge even the clipper ships.

Post Office Mail

The Post Office helped the new steamship companies by giving them contracts to carry Post Office mail.

The transatlantic contract was given to Samuel Cunard who had four steamships; the *Britannia, Arcadia, Caledonia* and *Columbia.*

By 1837 Willcox and Anderson had set up a monthly mail service to Gibraltar. Their company was the Peninsular Steam Navigation Company. In 1840 their contract was extended to Alexandria to form the Peninsular and Orient Company (P. and O.). During the next twenty years mail contracts helped to extend the steamship services across the world's sea lanes.

In 1856 the Union Steamship Company (Union Castle Line) received a mail contract, and in the 1860's the Blue Funnel Line was established. With cheaper sea travel available more ships were needed. There developed a distinction between cargo and passenger ships, and special liners were built. Steamships became even more reliable when they were built of steel and when twin screw-propellers were introduced. The first steel ship was the *Servia* in 1881.

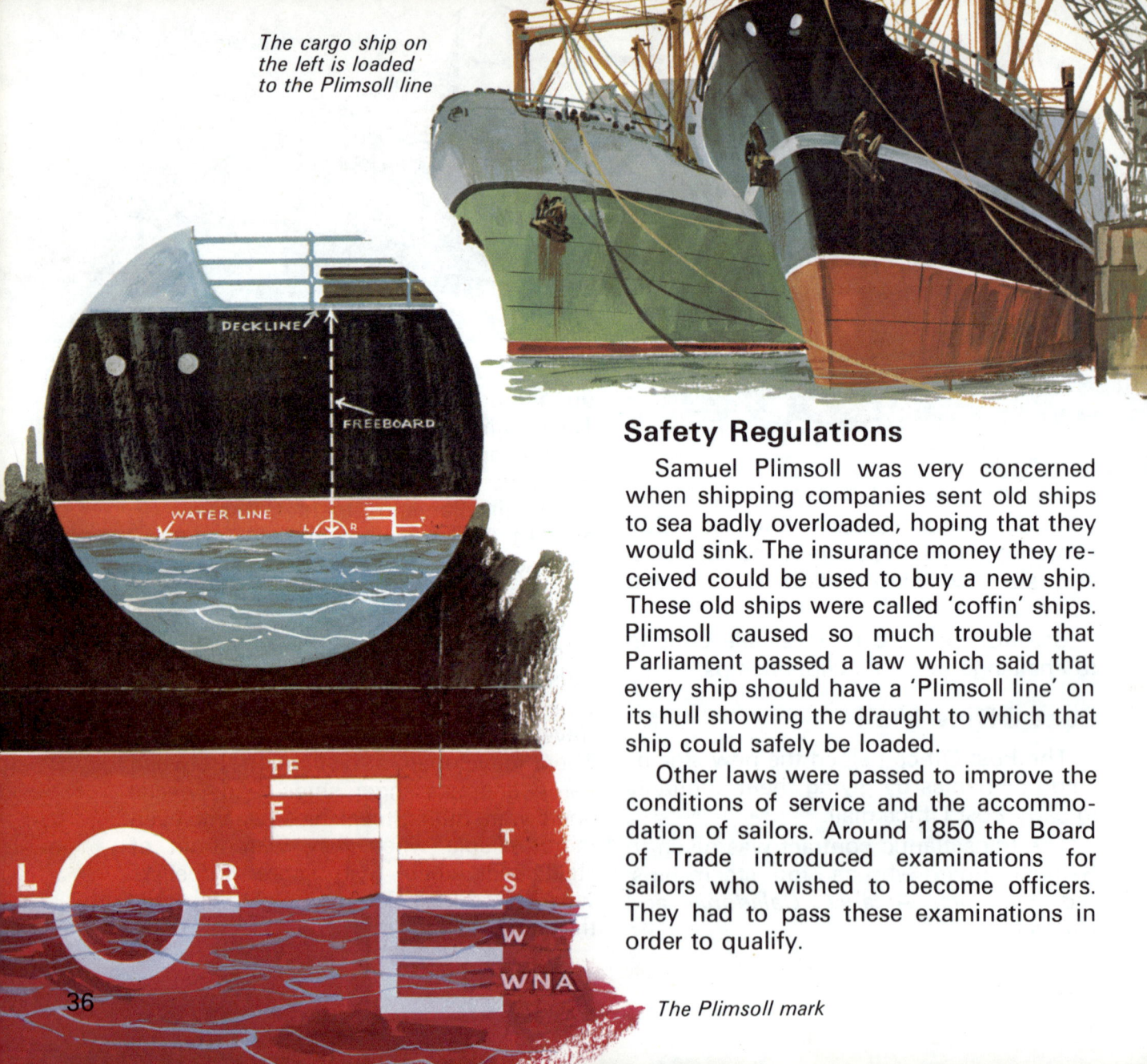

The cargo ship on the left is loaded to the Plimsoll line

DECKLINE

FREEBOARD

WATER LINE

Safety Regulations

Samuel Plimsoll was very concerned when shipping companies sent old ships to sea badly overloaded, hoping that they would sink. The insurance money they received could be used to buy a new ship. These old ships were called 'coffin' ships. Plimsoll caused so much trouble that Parliament passed a law which said that every ship should have a 'Plimsoll line' on its hull showing the draught to which that ship could safely be loaded.

Other laws were passed to improve the conditions of service and the accommodation of sailors. Around 1850 the Board of Trade introduced examinations for sailors who wished to become officers. They had to pass these examinations in order to qualify.

The Plimsoll mark

Iron Warships

Iron was also used in warships. Guns which fired high explosive shells could easily destroy and set fire to wooden warships. In 1859 the French constructed the first ironclad warship, the *Gloire*, whose sides were covered with thick bands of iron.

The following year the British Admiralty launched the first all-iron, screw-driven warship. She was the *Warrior*. She still carried her full complement of rigging, masts and sails.

The superiority of the iron warship was proved in the American Civil War, when the Confederate ship, the *Merrimack*, destroyed many Northern wooden warships before it met the *Monitor*.

The first modern-looking warship was launched by Britain in 1872. She was the *Devastation*. She had no rigging or sails and her breech-loading guns were mounted in movable turrets on the deck.

Warrior

Monitor

Devastation

37

Steam Turbine

In 1897 Charles Parsons took his ship the *Turbinia* to the British Naval Review at Spithead. The *Turbinia*, powered by a steam turbine, astonished everyone by her speed and manoeuvrability as she defied the attempts of the fastest warship to catch her.

The Admiralty ordered two destroyers with turbine engines, the *Viper* and the *Cobra*. From now on all warships were to have turbines.

In 1906 Britain launched a battleship which became the model for all battleships until 1945. She was the *Dreadnought,* powered by steam turbines. She was 175 metres long and 27 metres wide, and she had ten huge guns mounted in turrets, as well as five torpedo tubes.

The turbine engine was also used on passenger ships. The first steam turbine, the *Victorian*, was launched in 1904 and the first steam turbine ship to cross the Atlantic was the *Virginian*.

Turbinia

Dreadnought

Blue Riband Trophy

Mauretania

United States

The Blue Riband

The ship which crossed the Atlantic in the fastest time had the honour to hold the 'Blue Riband' of the Atlantic. The most famous holder of the Blue Riband was the *Mauretania* which held the record for twenty years. Liners continued to improve in speed and comfort, reaching the super-class of the huge luxury liners like the *Queen Mary* and *Queen Elizabeth*. The present holder of the 'Blue Riband' is the U.S.S. *United States*.

Improved Safety

The bows of ships are no longer upright but slope outwards. This reduces the risk of sinking in a collision, for the damage will occur above the water line.

Since 1905 radio has been used on ships and since the sinking of the *Titanic* a wireless operator must be on duty all the time.

The 'echo-sounder' fitted to the bottom of the ship automatically records the depth of the water, while the 'gyro compass' gives direction accurately and makes automatic steering possible. The development of 'radar' has also increased safety at sea.

Different methods of propulsion have also been developed. In 1910 the first ship with an engine burning diesel oil was launched. By 1918 there were many oil-burning ships. Motor-driven ships also appeared in the 1920's.

The S.S. *Normandie*, launched in 1932, was driven by turbo-electric power. Today there are few ships which still use coal.

As aircraft have developed, speed on the sea has become less important. People travelling by sea are more concerned with luxury and comfort.

Passenger liners like the *Canberra* and the *Queen Elizabeth 2* are designed for winter cruising as well as liner service. They have air-conditioned cabins, play-rooms for children, swimming pools, ball-rooms, cinema, television, radio, and lounges and restaurants.

But with fewer people travelling by sea many ships combine passenger carrying with cargo. Between two and three hundred passengers can be accommodated on these ships with every possible comfort and cargo is carried below deck.

Deck swimming pool

Canberra

Queen Elizabeth 2

Container ship

Cut-away of tanker

Tanker

Modern Cargo Liners

Cargo ships which sail on regular routes to a regular time-table are called liners. Ships to carry special types of cargo have been developed.

Among the most striking of modern cargo ships are the super-tankers which carry huge cargoes of crude oil or petroleum.

'Bulk-carriers' transport large cargoes of grain, iron-ore, coal and sugar.

Refrigeration ships carry fruit, meat, butter and eggs. Some ships are specially built to transport railway locomotives and large machinery which cannot be loaded through a normal hatchway. Car ferries and train ferries allow drivers to drive straight on board ship.

General cargo ships, sometimes called 'tramps', carry a wide variety of goods, from pins to tractors.

The most modern cargo ship is the 'container' ship. These ships are specially built to hold metal boxes which are of a standard size. The boxes can be clipped together to save space. Goods are packed in these containers and can remain there until they reach their destination.

41

Supplementary Shipping

There are now so many ships sailing the seas that special ships are needed to keep the sea lanes safe.

Icebreakers and dredgers clear the sea lanes of obstructions. Ocean-going tugs rescue ships in distress, and harbour tugs attend to large ships in port. Lightships give warning of danger, and weather ships give warning of bad weather. Lifeboats rush to the rescue of sailors in distress.

Fishing Fleets

'Drifters' are small fishing boats which do not make long sea voyages. Their nets are kept near the surface by means of cork floats. Fish are caught as the ship drifts along.

'Trawlers' are bigger and sometimes sail as far as Greenland. The trawler drags a huge net along the sea bed, scooping up the fish.

Some fishermen hunt whales. Their ships, called 'whalers', have harpoon guns to kill the whales. The whales are taken to a 'factory ship'.

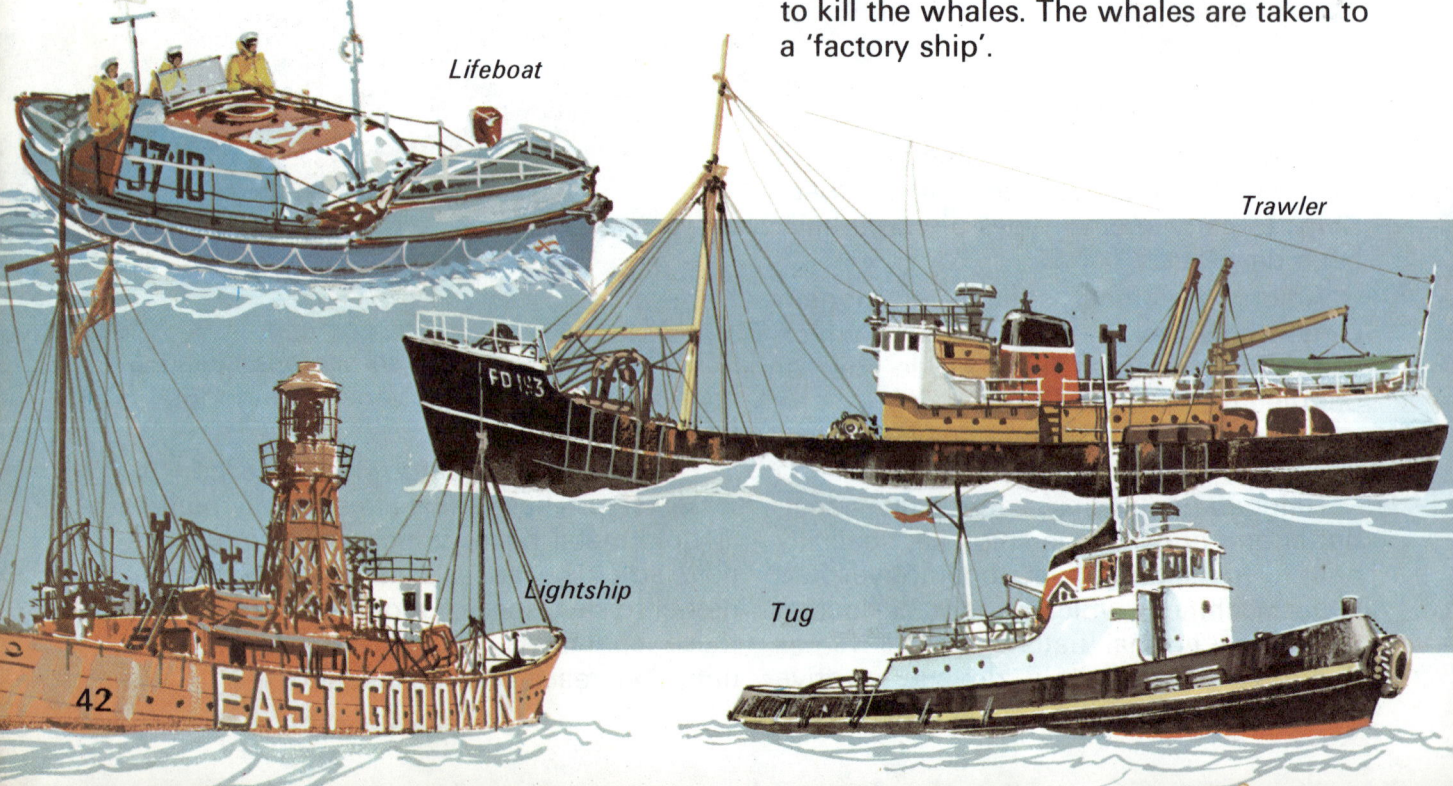

Lifeboat

Trawler

Lightship

Tug

42

EAST GOODWIN

Submarines

Early 'submarines' were designed by a Dutchman, Cornelius Drebbel, in the seventeenth century and by De Son, a Frenchman. However, the first real submarine was developed by David Bushnell, an American. His *Turtle* was egg-shaped and held one man. He turned the propeller by hand, while he operated a valve to let water in to sink his craft, and a hand pump to pump air out.

The development of the submarine was held up because of the lack of a suitable engine to drive it when underwater.

In 1863 the French Navy built *Le Plongeur* which was powered by compressed air, and in 1879 Garrett, an Englishman and a priest by profession, built the *Resurgam* which was driven by steam. Nordenfelt, a gunmaker, also built steam-driven underwater craft.

An American, named Holland, designed the modern submarine. His *Plunger* had two engines; a steam engine to drive it on the surface and an electric motor to power it when underwater. Later, he changed the steam engine for a gas engine.

In 1900 he sold his ninth submarine, the *Holland,* to the United States Navy. She had a petrol engine and an electric motor.

The Royal Navy adopted the Holland submarine.

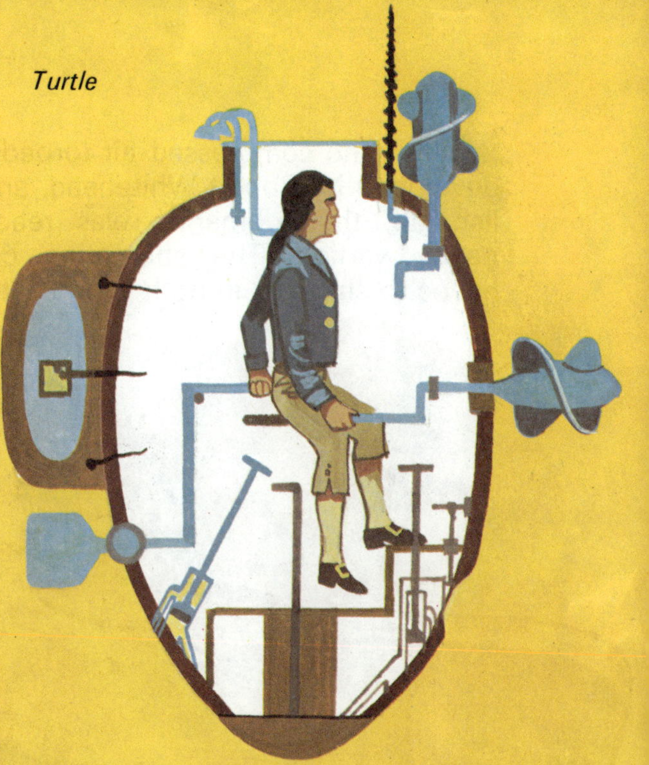

Turtle

Resurgam

43

When the compressed-air torpedo was developed by Robert Whitehead, an Englishman, the submarine was ready for naval warfare. The submarine created havoc to shipping in both World Wars.

In 1954 the Americans launched the first nuclear-powered submarine, the *Nautilus*. Its engine needs no air and she can stay underwater for weeks at a time. This enabled the *Nautilus*, captained by Commander Anderson, to sail right under the ice-cap of the North Pole in August 1958. To do this, she sailed 2900 kilometres underwater in 96 hours.

The first British nuclear submarine, H.M.S. *Dreadnought* was commissioned in 1963.

German U-boat

British Submarine
World War II

Nautilus

Frigate

F104

Mine-sweeper

M115

Guided-missile ship

F82

Aircraft carrier

Modern Warships

The development of the submarine created new dangers for the 'battleship' which had to be screened by light ships such as 'destroyers' and 'cruisers'. During the First World War battleships were loth to put to sea for fear of submarines. In the Second World War aircraft hastened the end of the large battleship.

When the striking power of aircraft was realised, cruisers and cargo ships were converted to carry aircraft and specially designed 'aircraft carriers' were built. These ships have a long flight deck with work-shops and aircraft hangars beneath.

The aircraft carrier is the largest ship in a modern fleet. The rest of the fleet are much smaller: frigates, corvettes, sloops, destroyer escorts, anti-aircraft ships, sub-marine-killers, guided-missile ships, mine-sweepers, minelayers and landing craft. These are just a few of the wide variety of modern warships.

There are even smaller ships such as torpedo boats and air-sea rescue ships.

45

The Future

Future ships will be powered by nuclear energy. The first merchant ship to be driven by nuclear power was the *Savannah* in the United States in 1959. She was an experimental ship and cost 90 000 000 dollars to build. She could travel for over three years without refuelling but she is much too expensive to run at a profit.

Russia has had the nuclear-powered ice-breaker *Lenin* in service for several years, but she, too, is very expensive to run.

A much cheaper form of nuclear power will have to be discovered before all merchant ships are powered in this way.

Warships do not need to pay their way in the same way as cargo ships. The United States has a fleet of nuclear-powered submarines as well as several nuclear-powered destroyers.

The largest aircraft carrier in the world is the nuclear-powered *Enterprise*, commissioned in 1961. She can stay at sea for five years without refuelling.

Savannah

Enterprise

Lenin

The voyage of the _Nautilus_ under the Polar ice-cap in 1958 pointed the way to the possible development of the use of submarines as cargo ships. The shortest route from the Pacific to the Atlantic is under the North Pole. A huge cargo submarine could take this route. Also, under water it would not be troubled by ice, fog or storms.

The cargo ship of the future could be a large nuclear-powered submarine, able to glide safely beneath the waves.

INDEX

フランス的クラシック生活

ルネ・マルタン 著／高野麻衣 解説
René Martin / Takano Mai

PHP新書